# Grace and Courtesy
a picture guide for children and adults

Written and Illustrated by Alicia Olson

Center for Children and Theology
www.cctheo.org
Washington DC

# DEDICATION

To Catherine Maresca whose encouragement brought this book to completion.

Author and illustrator Alicia Olson has also created *The Peace Rose*, and is the illustrator for *The Seed of God*. She lives in Michigan with her husband and two daughters and has been a Montessori teacher since 2001.

I am respectful.

I talk with a soft voice.

I walk with careful feet.

I can say, "Please walk around my mat."

I carry my work with two strong hands.

I walk by friends without interrupting their work.

I treat materials gently.

When I work by a friend I focus on my own work.

I kindly say, "Please don't disturb my work."

I put my work away and make it beautiful for the next person.

I roll up my mat for the next person to use.

I sit up at group with my legs crossed and my hands in my lap.

I know, one person talks at a time.

When I need to get by someone I say, "Excuse me."

I hold the door for the next person.

I treat others how I want to be treated.

# Introducing Grace and Courtesy Lessons to Children

Young children are deeply fascinated by the ways in which people around them interact. They are drawn to becoming an active and contributing part of their social community. Dr. Montessori said, "It is interesting to see how, little by little, [the children] become aware of forming a community which behaves as such. They come to feel part of a group to which their activity contributes. And not only do they begin to take an interest in this, but they work on it profoundly, as one may say, in their hearts. Once they have reached this level, the children no longer act thoughtlessly, but put the group first and try to succeed for its benefit." (Montessori, 1995, p. 232.)

One of the ways we help the child in the development of social cohesion is through the lessons of Grace and Courtesy. The lessons of Grace and Courtesy are designed to promote harmony in the very broadest sense—harmony between mind and body, and harmony between ourselves and others. The focus of these lessons is on a way of moving or speaking in a specific social situation—hoping this will help the child to feel comfortable with herself and with other people.

These lessons are given to a small group of children, at a neutral time. The teacher might say, "I'm going to pretend that I'm 3-years-old. I need to get to the map on the shelf, but Julia is blocking my way. Listen to what I say to Julia when she is blocking my way." With a willing child as a volunteer, the teacher, simply and directly, acts out the words she'd use in the situation. "Julia, excuse me. Can I get to the shelf?" Afterwards, the teacher invites other children to act out the situation. They take great delight in practicing how to handle this social interaction by themselves.

Once a Grace and Courtesy lesson has been given formally, usually near the beginning of the year, the pictures in the book can serve as a visual reminder. Choose one page, and leave it up for the day.

— Kristi Medley

The lessons of Grace and Courtesy in Montessori environments that replace "classroom management" help children to build community together. Simple sentences and related art will guide you through the lessons of Grace and Courtesy and serve as a gentle reminder of the practices that create harmony among children.

www.cctheo.org

$12.00
ISBN 978-0-9819345-5-6